THE CRAB SYNDROME

Antuan Simmons

ii

To the readers of The Crab Syndrome.

From my heart to your thoughts.

-Antuan Simmons

Copyright©2007-2012 by Antuan Rene' Simmons. All rights reserved, printed in the United States of America. No part of this book may be reproduced in any manner whatsoever without permission, except in case of brief quotations embodied in critical articles and reviews. For information email goodpoetry29@yahoo.com.

Acknowledgements

First off, all glory goes to God, this book would not be possible without you, thanks for listening to my prayers at night.

DJ KIDD- Thanks for the running commercials for my last book. Every time I needed radio advertisements you were always there, I appreciate that.

Shon and Maxx- Thank for doing those internet videos for me.

Martin and Jamil- Thanks for coming out to Hastings Books and Music and filming my performance, that was cool.

Mrs. Dorothy- Thanks for your time and patience. I appreciate that you took special care of my books, it was important to me.

Maurice G- Thanks for giving me a chance to show my poetry talents at your club and bringing Maurice G entertainment, and all the comedians to Wichita Falls.

Monique Bruner- Thanks for inviting me to all the literary functions in Oklahoma City, and being so professional to where I always felt comfortable.

Wichita Falls Hastings Books and Music- Thanks for hosting my book signings.

Mannie, Bruce, Searchin- Thanks for bringing me into your Lawton poetry world, I learned a lot from you guys. I finally realized the power of the spoken word. I thought I would have to search far, but you all were just 45 minutes away.

Wichita Falls Public Library (Librarians: Eric, Kim, Andrew, Don, and Deanna,) Thanks for answering my questions and helping me out with my computer problems. You all take the word librarian to a new level. I see it now as a person of great knowledge and expertise, and that is how I see you guys. Every library I go to I expect them to be good as you all.

To all the great overnight staff at Wal- Mart 1148, you kept the shift filled with joy and laughter; I grew as a person because of you guys, I won't forget you all.

Douglas and Marylin Simmons (Mom and Dad). Thanks for all your support through the two years of writing this book.

Chastity Smith and Chianti McGee, thanks for taking the time out to proof read the extra poems I put in

Table of Contents

Acknowledgements

Crab Mentality

This World Is Oh So Strange

My People

All Walks Of Life

Conquer Your Fears

Why You Are My Valentine

Your Biggest Fan

Download It Into My Head-A Story

Will You Love Me When I Am No Longer Famous?

Celebrate My Death, Celebrate My Funeral

What Wichita Falls Was Like Before Hot 103.9

The People Behind The Glass

My Friend Called DOPE

Collapsing

The Coming Of Christ

The Haters

A Preacher's Story

What If Superman Never Had A Clark Kent?

Reasons Why I Love My Mother

Respect

The Lord's Discipline

12 Reasons why people HATE!

The Looking Glass

Forever With You

Past, Present, Future

10 Reasons Why Women Become Strippers?

As They Say...It's All Bullshit

Fame

Let's Come Together To Celebrate Juneteenth

Making Love In The Matrix

Pinch My Nipples

I Go Quietly

Yes, I Will Love You When You Are No Longer Famous.

The Crab Syndrome

Crab Mentality

Describes a way of thinking best described by the phrase if I can't have it, neither can you." The metaphor refers to a pot of crabs in which one tries to escape over the side, but is relentlessly pulled down by the others in the pot.

This term is broadly associated with short-sighted, non-constructive thinking rather than a unified, long-term, constructive mentality. It is also often used colloquially in reference to individuals or communities attempting to "escape" a so-called "underprivileged life", but kept from doing so by those others of the same community or nation attempting to ride upon their coattails.

This World Is Oh So Strange

The world is calm, the world is chaotic.

In the words of Erykah Badu, this world is oh so strange.

Indeed a strange world, but it is neither to the rich or poor, wise or foolish, but to the one who found joy in it.

My People

My brother, don't leave me.

My brother, don't kill me.

Shine a light so I can see.

Don't tell me to have small dreams.

Don't call me a fool.

Don't tell me that I cannot make it.

Don't tell me I won't amount to anything.

Don't tell me that I am not good enough.

Don't kick me when I am down.

Don't tell me it is not my place.

Tell me my life is worth something.

Help me stand when I fall.

Inspire me, encourage me.

Don't be jealous of me.

Don't laugh at me.

Tell me right, don't tell me wrong.

Don't give up on me.

Don't kill my spirit.

Motivate me.

Don't shatter me.

My brother, don't leave me.

My brother, don't kill me.

Don't leave me here in the dark.

Shine a light so I can see.

If you help me, I'll help you.

If you give me a hand, I'll give you two.

If you support me, I'll support you.

If you're real with me, I'll be real with you.

My brother.

Don't leave me here in the dark.

Shine a light so I can see.

My sister, don't leave me.

My sister, don't kill me.

Don't leave me here in the dark.

Shine a light so I can see.

Don't compare me to other men.

Don't compare me to the men that did you wrong.

Don't judge me before you know me.

Don't put my every mistake under a microscope.

Don't break me down, build me up.

Don't be negative, be positive.

Help me find my dreams.

Help me have hope for another day.

Don't tell me that I am less than a man.

Don't be bitter.

Don't destroy me with gossip.

Don't be hateful

Don't cause other women to be disgusted with men.

Don't be miserable.

Love us men, forgive us men, have compassion on us men.

Support us men who are trying to do right.

If you help me, I'll help you.

If you give me a hand, I'll give you two.

If you support me, I'll support you.

If you're real with me, I'll be real with you.

My people.

I am the son struggling in society.

The father trying to raise his family.

The uncle who is trying to manage his health.

The nephew who just graduated.

I am a man who needs help from his People.

My people, don't leave me.

My people, don't kill me.

Don't leave me here in the dark.

Shine a light so I can see.

All Walks Of Life

What do you want out of life?

In my life I have seen all walks of life, and I ask myself, where am I or who am I in the middle of all this?

How much do I let society control my life, who I want to be or where I want to go?

This world is filled with so much influence.

It is such a struggle between who society says I am, and who I really want to be.

The struggle to live life their way or my way. How much do I have to sacrifice to achieve what I'm destined for?

How much will I gain or how much will I lose?

How much is worth the risk?

In my life I have seen all kinds of people, from all walks of life.

In life I have seen

The ambitious

The haters

The sex fiends

The freaks

The wannabes

The know-it-alls

The healers

The destroyers

The artists

The musicians

The workaholics

The controlling

The warm hearted

The beggars.

The listeners

The jealous

The conceited

The ego maniacs

The greedy

The holier than thou

The patient

The kind

The wicked

The evil

The materialistic

The superficial

The attractive….

Everybody has a role on the stage of life. What role do you want to play?

Life has its heroes and villains.

There will always be players that are going to play, there will always be haters that are going to hate.

There will always be shot callers that are going to call.

There will always be the wealthy and rich, the poor and oppressed.

They don't have anything to do with how you want to live your life.

People have been the same since the beginning of human civilization, the way it is, it has always been.

The names have changed, but it's still the same people in the game.

Ecclesiastes 1:9 Says "What has been will be again, what has been done will be done again."

What do you want or who you want to be in life? What character do you want to play?

You are born, you live, and you die. What do you want to do with the time in between?

There has always been,

The beautiful

The ugly

The outcast

The less fortunate

The shunned

The charming

The users

The manipulators

The ignorant

The foolish

The lost

The mad

The immature

The emotional

The moody

The passionate

The devious

The womanizers

The liars

The generous

The faithful

The pompous

The ambitious

The wicked

The arrogant

The snobbish

The disciplined

The winners

The losers

The genuine

The humble

The sheltered

The spoiled

The sincere

The analytical

The perfectionist

The heartless

The studious

The leaders

The followers

The peacemakers

The war mongers

The virgins

The whores

The virtuous

The hypocrites

The nagging

The easygoing

The sociable

The socialites

The powerful

The weak

The useless

The easily influenced

The self-indulgent

The opinionated

The reckless

The lazy

The conniving

The trustworthy

The rich

The poor

The determined

The lustful

The suicidal

The self-destructive

The sick

The optimistic

The humorous

The pessimistic

The miserable

The perverted

The loner

The attention getter

The eccentric

The talented

The weak-willed

The unforgiving

The forgettable

The unforgettable

Everybody has a role on the stage of life.

What role do you want to play?

Life has its heroes and villains.

There will always be players that are going to play, there will always be haters that are going to hate.

There will always be shot callers that are going to call.

There will always be the wealthy and rich, the poor and oppressed.

They don't have anything to do with how you want to live your life.

People have been the same since the beginning of human civilization, the way it is, it has always been.

The names have changed, but it's still the same people

in the game.

Ecclesiastes 1:9 Says "What has been will be again, what has been done will be done again."

What do you want or who you want to be in life? What character do you want to play?

You are born, you live and you die. What do you want to do with the time in between?

What do you want out of life?

If you make it to old age and you look back at the years you have lived, whose life would you have wanted to live, yours or someone else's?

Conquer Your Fears

Fear turns a swimming pool into an ocean.

Turns moments into countless hours, and makes something easy into something difficult.

It turns a simple unraveling of a rope into a knot that you eventually have to throw away.

If you would have just relaxed and had no tension, the knot would have easily slipped, uncoiled, and become undone practically by itself.

The more fear you had, the tighter the knot became.

Fear turns a walk across the street into a canyon trek.

A pebble into a boulder.

A ladder into a mountain.

Fear multiplies and enhances, it turns that simple 20-pound weight into a massive ton.

Fear is that born instinct/sense that keeps you as a caterpillar or can burst you into flight like a colorful butterfly.

It keeps a great singer, into a person who just had a great voice in the neighborhood.

A great scientist into a person who just like hanging around a lab.

It keeps a great orator that wrote speeches, but never practiced them.

A great magician who learned a couple of tricks, but never did get that rabbit into the hat.

A great president who only got as far as the debate class.

Fear keeps us from danger, but it also keeps us from tapping into our full potential.

Fear is frightening, horrific, terrifying, and embarrassing, and you might even look like an utter fool.

If you can break down the wall of fear you can be…

The singer who becomes the number 1 artist;

The Nobel Prize winner;

The lauded lecturer;

The illusionist;

One of the greatest Presidents of all time.

Only you know how tall your measuring stick stands, and every foot there is a fear to overcome.

Every fear you overcome only brings you higher.

Higher faith in yourself.

Higher belief in your abilities and talents.

Higher confidence and self-esteem in yourself.

Lastly, an opportunity to have a great life that would have never been possible if you never conquered your fears.

Why You Are My Valentine

Very positive when things were negative.

Always encouraging me, lifting me up with inspiration and support, and not criticizing me when I did things wrong.

Each dream, you told me, was just a reality waiting to be built.

Never listen to people who do not believe in your dreams. Do not listen to people who do not dream.

Ideas were impossible things made possible, with will power, patience, motivation, prayer and great follow up.

Nothing was created into something without a thought, a dream, or an idea.

Everything built was at one time a dream.

Every failure, disappointment, bad choice, loss, and utter disaster, you stuck by me.

That is why you are my valentine.

Your Biggest Fan

(*Words in Italics*-Is the woman speaking.)

Do you believe in me?

I don't know?

Baby I know times are hard right now I know money is tight, but I got to see this business through. I know I *ain't* got much money, but soon…stay.

Baby when we first met, you was bigger than life. You were, to all the other poets, a sun compared to a lit candle. Everybody else was just fireflies, you were beautiful and magical.

I was drawn to your strength, your fearlessness, your light. You touched my every nerve ending, your words were a mental climax rippling through me.

You completed me, you filled that void every woman wants in a man. You gave me that amazement, that wonderment, that firmament. An earth angel, less than God, but more than man.

You were struggling, I knew that, I accepted that, but I

23

thought that you were close to making it.

You were too good for the industry to not want you.

We met at one of your shows, I surprised you by reciting a poem for you. Mixed with some of your own words recited from memory, blew you away.

You asked me out on a date. Six weeks later I became your girl. I loved you. I was your ace, your main supporter, your promoter, your lover. We were a team.

I made sacrifices; I know that you did too. I was in school, about to graduate. I spent hours promoting your art on Myspace, Twitter, and Facebook. After that I would study until I fell asleep.

Pass out flyers to student organizations, setting up shows. Traveling miles to other cities, barely making it to class to take tests.

Missing plans with friends, not able to spend time with my family. You were my man, and I was your biggest fan, I loved you.

Baby I understand the sacrifices, it takes normally five years to start a business, something will happen.

I made calls to club owners, and bookings to have me as a feature. I called 20 radio DJ's, newspapers, and TV stations.

I made a little money at the last show, you were there. All those 10, 20, 50, 100 dollar bills, the crowd showed loved.

I got a standing ovation. Baby the struggle will be over, we will look back and laugh at all this, I need for you to be here…baby.

I know about the money coming in from your shows, but it's not consistent. One show you might make a grand, another you might sell one CD.

It's not a steady income.

You might pay the rent, but have nothing for the car bill, might have enough for the car bill, but have nothing for the utilities.

This is a hit and miss lifestyle. Baby, I paid your rent last time.

You almost got evicted!

Do you think that it is worth it?

Yes, I do.

All this struggle?

Yes, I think it is worth it, it is what I do, I do poetry, and music.

Baby why don't you go to school, enroll at the university. I know some students on campus, some professors, they could help you.

The academia doesn't accept street poets.

Do you believe in me?

Can you see yourself doing this in 20 years?

I would have made it by then.

How do you know!!!!

In this world, without a college degree, the chances of making a decent income are slim.

You didn't always talk like this.

Until I saw how great the struggle was. How much you struggled, how much we struggled.

The competition is fearless, how picky the industry can be. They rather pick sex and vulgarity, over spirituality.

Baby I am throwing in the towel. I have done my rounds, tired of taking punches, getting bruised.

So what are you saying?

This guy asked me out. He has a bachelor's degree and he is going to law school in the fall.

Baby please.

He is stable, predictable, supportive, and reliable.

What happened to the woman that I first met?

I've grown, I cannot dream when I am tired and hungry. I need to be free, and this man can release me.

(She touches his face)

I wish you luck great poet, I hope your music inspires not only you, but everyone around you.

I hope you find what you are looking for, and find great respect in what you do.

I hope God finds favor in your words and poetry.

You are a beautiful person, but this world is not ready for beauty. It wants lust, sex, greed, money, and power, this world is too selfish.

Your sun as bright as it was, is too weak for this black, dark, cold world, but things are ever changing.

As long as there is humanity, there will be poets.

Maybe your time is not now, maybe God is waiting to gather all the right people. Maybe He's teaching your patience.

Baby my patience has run out. I was not strong enough. I did not have the heart of an artist, to create whether hungry or full, applauded or shunned.

Your resilience to keep on going, only shows how beautiful you are.

Keep that close to your heart, and you will always be a full person among empty people.

(She touches his cheek)

On your journey I hope you find someone better than me, who could be a good wife, a good mother. So you do not have to share your poetry alone.

(Kisses him)

Now and until my dying day, every book you write, I will buy and read it. Every music CD, I will listen to. I will support you, even if I am not with you.

Remember, wherever you are, and wherever I am, I will always and forever be your biggest fan.

(Kisses him again, turns around, and walks away.)

Download It Into My Head-A Story

The great discovery has been made.

They can now download information from the internet into a person's brain.

One of the greatest discoveries of the century.

Lomax Sinclair, one of the scientists who created this new device called "the cerebral link" is the first successful recipient.

We asked Sinclair a couple of questions.

"Mr. Sinclair, how are you able to get information from the internet to your brain, and what are the benefits of cerebral link or cerebral download?"

Sinclair stated, "This is a great technology, no more does man have to regurgitate or memorize any information. The information just passes from the computer to the brain through a cord that is plugged into the lower base of the skull. It can also be done wirelessly."

"Mr. Sinclair, are there any drawbacks or flaws?"

Sinclair stated, "None whatsoever."

As the weeks passed Sinclair did lectures, and demonstrations of the cerebral device.

He performed mathematical calculations, and solved numerous problems. He could answer any questions via the skull to internet link.

The cerebral device began being mass produced and marketed.

Thousands of people were volunteering to put a hole in the back of their head.

During one of Sinclair's lectures a hand was raised.

Sinclair answered, "Yes sir."

"Mr. Sinclair I am Jacob Jaakar from the Institute of Beta Robotics and Artificial Intelligence."

Sinclair answered, "Yes, what is your question?"

"Me and my colleague's think your cerebral invention has flaws, and should be reconsidered going into mass production."

Sinclair stated, "Mr. Jakaar my invention is full proof,

we ran numerous tests."

Jaakar said, "Then I will challenge you to a test of minds, my human mind against your cyborg mind."

Sinclair said, "That is cerebral mind, and I will accept your challenge."

As the weeks follow, it is announced throughout the world of Sinclair and Jakaar challenge, the headlines reading "Man Against Machine!"

The whole world was in awe, and they questioned, how can a mere man win against a man that can download information into his head via the internet?

The day came and thousands arrived, millions watched.

The first question was asked.

"What is 15 times 15?"

Sinclair and Jakaar both answered, "225."

The second question was asked,

"What is 1575 times 1325?"

Jakaar answered, "I do not know from the top of my

head."

The question was re-asked to Sinclair, his eyes started flickering and his head drew back, as he downloaded the answer.

Sinclair answered, "2086875!"

The judge said, "Mr. Sinclair you are right!"

As the contest went on, Sinclair was winning at most of the questions, defeating Mr. Jakaar flawlessly.

It went on for about an hour and the world knew who the winner will be.

The next question "What was the operating system used before Vista?"

Jakaar answered "Windows XP!"

Sinclair answered with his eyes flickering and rolling back in his head to download the answer. He answered, "Windo…..Windooo….Windooos… A h....I…I…Ahhh….Am…Ahhhhhh….. I'm….a wild and crazy guy,…Immm..aaa. Willldd..annd….crazy…Guuuy!"

Then all of a sudden Sinclair started dancing and

crossing his legs together. With his hands back and forth shouting, "Imm…a…wild…and…crazy…guy..!" Then he fell down and passed out. The crowd was stunned.

"What happened!"

There was silence.

Jakaar answered, "Me and my colleagues simply hacked into the cerebral device. It took us a while, we had to follow the connection from the computer to the brain. It took some time to get passed the firewall. We thought we had to hack the base computer, but we had to get passed the skull implant also. His security was good, but we got around that. My colleagues were a couple of feet away recording his movements. Once we hacked into it, we added some commentary from the comedian Steve Martin. Mr. Sinclair will be okay in a couple of minutes".

He continued, "We just wanted to show if we can hack into it, others can too. What if this device was mass produced, and giving to thousands of unsuspecting people waiting for their minds to be taken over? There needs to be better and tighter security measures. Mr. Sinclair has a brilliant idea, but of course, he never imagined the darker element to use it for evil."

34

Jakaar added, "We want to help Mr. Sinclair by developing a better cerebral device and I hope he welcomes our request."

Suddenly Mr. Sinclair wakens, "Whaaatt…happened?"

"It is a long story Mr. Sinclair (helps him up). Jakaar and his group just proved that your invention is in need of assistance."

"Mr. Sinclair teams and Mr. Jakaar teams work together to improve the cerebral device so that it benefit's the betterment of humankind."

Moral of the story-When will man add technology to increase his intellect. How cautious or careless will we be?

Will You Love Me When I Am No Longer Famous?

When the lights have died down, and the applause has come to an end.

When the fans stop their clapping sounds, and I walk down the stage to my final descend.

When they cease to ask for autographs, my personal signatures on hats, blouses, and jerseys.

No more invitations, parties, drinks, and laughs, when my name is no longer important in the industry.

Will you love me when I am no longer famous, when they no longer cheer for me?

Will you love me when I am no longer famous, when they no longer clap for me?

Will you love me when I am no longer famous, when my name no longer causes an uproar?

Will you love me when I am no longer famous, when they no longer ask for an encore?

Will you love me when I am no longer famous? When they no longer roll out the red carpet, no more camera flashes taken by fans?

No more limousine rides or thousand dollar outfits, no more crying faces when they shake my hand.

When my Hollywood status becomes low, as I enter into common reality?

No more agents, deals, or performing shows, when they see me more as a person, and less as a celebrity?

As I pass away like a fad, undress me like an outdated trend. Let go of the things I had, lose contact with my closest friends.

New stars come to take my place, and they will relive what I had done.

The new talent, trend, fad, and face, and they will have their moment in the celebrity sun.

Will you love me when I am no longer famous, when they no longer cheer for me?

Will you love me when I am no longer famous, when they no longer clap for me?

Will you love me when I am no longer famous, when
my name no longer causes an uproar?

Will you love me when I am no longer famous, when
they no longer ask for an encore?

Will you love me when I am no longer famous? Will it
be us and we, as the glitz and glow is left behind?

As former friends stop speaking to me, and the bank
account drops a little each time.

Can you stand not being in the spotlight, no more phone
calls from media giants?

No more image to hide behind, getting no attention
from others sight.

Can you live without the glamour's life, normalcy, could
you find it?

Could you run away with me? Forget the luxury cars,
coats, mansions, articles in newspapers.

Us and we, maybe start a family? Could we live
without the chefs, personal assistants, and waiters?

Could you look and say, "I still love this person, for all
that they are trying to become, and trying to be?"

With or without the pearls, diamonds, big houses, boats interior decorator, and fancy curtains?

If I lose it all tomorrow, will you still be around? If I lose it today, how upset would you be?

Would you pick me up when I was down, or would you, leave me?

Will you love me when I am no longer famous, when they no longer cheer for me?

Will you love me when I am no longer famous, when they no longer clap for me?

Will you love me when I am no longer famous, when my name no longer causes an uproar?

Will you love me when I am no longer famous, when they no longer ask for an encore?

Will you love me when I am no longer famous?

Celebrate My Death, Celebrate My Funeral

Do not weep for me at my death. Do not weep for me at my funeral.

Cheer at my death. Cheer at my funeral.

I am away from life's pain. No more heartaches and heartbreaks.

I am away from the meanness of the general public.

No more paying bills, no more flus, colds, or getting sick.

Celebrate my death, celebrate my funeral.

At my funeral, do not wear black, wear white.

With satin, silk, and rayon. Dressed snow from head to toe.

I want my casket to be white like ivory (I did not say made of ivory).

With gold trimmings (even if it is fake gold, as long as it shines).

I want jazz music playing in the air. On the other side keep it Krunk.

Wear top hats and long suits, bring your cane.

Stacey Adams, and Wing tips, Sean John, Prada, Baby Phat, Fubu, and Roca Wear, starched jeans with a deep crease.

Clean off your favorite athletic shoes.

Wear your jewelry, wear your gold.

Have your face grilled up, have your hair trimmed, and your hair braided.

During the service, serve barbecue, candy yams, potato salad, and cherry pies.

Have a keg of beer in the back, have waiters and waitresses serve everybody.

Serve coleslaw, buttered rolls, collard greens, hot links, ribs, drumsticks, a big mixed salad, chocolate cake, fruit salad, and broccoli rice casserole, and brisket.

The drinkers sip on Coors, Budweiser or beer of choice.

While the others sip on Kool-Aid, punch, and tea.

Yeah, be buzzed at my funeral, yeah be tipsy at my funeral.

Be full at my funeral, Have a good time at my funeral.

This is the best way to remember me.

Again, I said do not weep at my funeral.

If you need to cry, go ahead and cry, but do not mourn at my funeral.

There is nothing to be sad about if you believe in an afterlife.

For those who believe in a God we will meet again someday.

Celebrate my death, celebrate my funeral.

Tip your drink, eat your barbecue.

Play Tupac's "Life Goes On". And bury me with a smile from cheek to cheek.

Because I am "out of here!"

Do not weep or mourn for me

What Wichita Falls Was Like Before Hot 103.9

Authors Note: They say a city is only as good as its music. If anybody understands this poem, you are showings of your age.

When everybody wanted to rule the world with Tears for Fears, my block listened to Doug E. Fresh and the Get Fresh Crew.

While Huey Lewis and The News played in our ear, Lodi Dodi, The Show, and Dana Dane are all we knew.

The local radio station played Top 40 hits, surrounded in a circle we watched B.E.T on the screen.

George Michael and Michael Bolton were on top of music charts.

While the Adventures of Slick Rick was number one in Jet magazine.

Hip-hop never came to a Wichita Falls station. Digable Planets, Goodie Mob, De La Soul, Pharcyde, Tribe called Quest, and Guru you could not find.

"We built this city on Rock and Roll" from Starship played across the nation, heard that song about a thousand times.

Rebirth of slick (cool like dat), Bonita Apple bum Jazzmatazz, Cell therapy, and Potholes in my lawn, got no play.

This what Wichita Falls was like before Hot 103.9

Cable hooked up to a stereo system, antenna's tweaked and turned to perfect the reception.

After watching video soul, we would gain momentum to hear music from another city's station.

To listen to our style and taste, music we would buy.

Ladies going crazy Over Christopher Williams, Al B. Sure, Troop, Jodeci and Guy.

The 90's and the 80's when Pebbles drove her Mercedes.

Our harmony was not played on the airwaves. There was no reason to request a song on the phone.

Hip-hop, Pop, and R&B did not play in those days. We lived and worked in this city, but musically it was not our home.

If you did not have cable T.V or a stereo, you were musically deaf, dumb, blind, and behind the times.

By the time you heard the new music, it was 6 months old. This is what Wichita Falls was like before Hot 103.9.

Nobody talked about the local radio station. When we all had tapes, before C.D.'s, downloads, and Mp3's.

Everybody was jealous and hating on the guy who drove to Dallas to get the latest Hip-Hop and R&B.

Early Wichita had its own style. Depehe Mode, Bangles, New Kid's on the Block, Culture Club, Pet Shop Boys, Belinda Carlisle, Reo Speedwagon, Richard Marx, Eurhythmics was all hot.

I respect them all, I can't lie.

I bought a New Kids on the Block tape at the mall.

But what about the artists we never saw.

Big Daddy Kane, Biz Markie, Special Ed, Public Enemy and Boogie Down.

MC Lyte, Monie Love, Queen Latifah, Sistah Souljah, Yo-Yo, Boss, Lady of Rage brought the Ladies sound.

The Too Shorts, The Ice T's, The Heavy D's, And O.C's.

Outkast Hey Ya is loved by all, but I remember a time, when Player's Ball, did not come to Wichita Falls.

Our music, our style, our art.

Bleached jeans, painted overalls, the girls started wearing weaves. LL cool J wanted an around the way girl.

While she wanted a New Edition Bobby Brown, button on her sleeve. Hammer pants, Kwamane polka dots, our own little world.

The Chili bowl, The Gumby, Geometric haircuts, Orange dye streaks, Finger waves, and the Curl.

This is what Wichita Falls was like before Hot 103.9.

This is how Wichita Falls is now, our wish came from forever asking, a station to represent more of our crowd.

Hot 103.9 and Cumulus broadcasting.

Advertiser of our businesses, speaker of our politics. Promoter of our local recording artists, and the muse to our poets.

Our eyes, ears, and words to what we say voice to the community our Hot 103.9 DJ's.

If Wichita Falls can change, I guess there is hope for anything. I guess all good things come in time.

An example that Wichita Falls is actually moving, because of Cumulus broadcasting and Hot 103.9.

The People Behind The Glass

The people behind the glass were so odd to me.

Their ways, their deceitfulness, their trickery, their meanness. Their constant unhappiness with your life and the decisions that you made.

They love to create emotional and mental snares for others to fall into.

Vindictive. Breaking people down was their endorphin, their stimulant.

How they made it this far in life with this behavior, I don't know.

They wear the mask of a "good and nice", but are the wolf in sheep's clothing.

The people behind the glass. Do they ever change?

Their meanness is bonded to their bone, mixed in with their blood.

They love being the puppet god, to have others dance upon their strings.

Their perspective is only of an earthly existence.

Get what you can and use people while you live.

Did they know that they were behind the glass?

That they were the least of society.

"The Glass Wall" That thin line that separates how things are what and what they are not supposed to be.

But Alas! The years turned. I grew older.

Those who were honest, the caring, the compassionate, the hardworking.

Those who knew the struggle, and finds a way to make the struggling easier.

The ones with that welcoming smile.

The first to give, the last to take.

The better half of society.

These good people's glass wall was actually smaller, and the people on the other side, the wicked, that their glass wall was bigger, wider.

Do we inherently lean toward the darker side of humanity rather than the lighter?

Is it true in church hymns, and biblical scriptures, when they say numerous times that heaven is my home, and that earth is temporary, we are just passing through?

Don't get me wrong, earth is beautiful, but it's humans. Some are okay, the others tear the heart out of a person's chest.

Some people are born good and some are just born with evil traits. But all of us make the choice on how we want to live.

Do either accept or reject the conscience. The choice to do good or evil.

I found to my dismay. The glass reality was reversed.

I was in the glass cage, and the people behind the glass was on the other side. They were looking at me, and that my ways were so odd to them.

My goodness and kindness were nothing more than just weakness. Something to take advantage of.

"The Glass wall", that thin slit of reality of what things are and what they are not supposed to be.

Was the wide gate truly the path to destruction, and the narrow gate to righteousness?

To end this story, the people on my side of the glass were at peace. We were kind, but we stood our ground.

Knowing there is never true complete peace as long as you are walking on the earth. As much peace that the world could give. We had that peace that came from God.

That dazzle in dismal and glow in gloom.

The people on the other side of the glass loved the wickedness. Their tongues and ways caused their own downfalls.

Being mean and wicked was a normal everyday thing. To them it was just another day of life. It was how you were supposed to act to get by, to get what you wanted.

They tried to do good things to cover up their bad. Thinking that it would balance out.

Their bad outweighed their good.

The people on my side of the glass were respected and rewarded for simply being good and decent people. For being strong and not turning to the ways of darkness.

People respected us because we were good, hardworking and honest. They were some good people left in the world.

They could rely on someone to trust. Not everyone was bad, and dishonest. They appreciated us, because we tried to do right.

The people on the other side of the glass had fake friends, and their spirit eventually grew accustomed to doing wrong.

Yes, they had friends, but their friends only stayed around so they can get something from them.

As soon as they could not provide for their friends, that is when their friends disappeared.

They found know fault in deceiving others. Sadly, that is just the way they lived.

They were convinced that was a natural way a person should live.

Get what you can while you live.

The people behind the glass.

My Friend Called DOPE

"I come to you as a friend, but my intention is to make you my slave"

You were beautiful, and young.

Your eyes were so bright and clear like a glass star that could light up the darkest part of the planet.

Even the space shuttle could see you.

Everywhere you went, there was no such thing as night.

Your smile was bright, along with your halo.

Your body was built like the finest stallion, a thoroughbred.

You had the mind of Einstein. Bred for success in life.

You had all the right tools, brains, wit, charisma, plus willpower.

The Time magazine front cover type.

But, ...I had to get you.

You have always seen me throughout your life, but was too scared to come over and speak to me.

You always heard I was bad news.

Rumors scared you,….kept you away

But… your friends loved me.

They brought me along to parties, stashed me at the back of clubs. They had sooo much fun with me.

I was their friend they showed me around to everybody.

Even after all the bad things the books, psychologist, counselors, and newspapers said about me.

I was some tool of Satan.

Bump that!

I made the fun funnier, the happy happier, and the situation better.

I made men and women impervious and invulnerable.

I took their minds off of stress.

A little snort, a little smoke, a little pop here and there. I was their friend.

A friend called DOPE.

….. ….. …..

You happened to be at one of their parties, I recognized you.

Bright eyed and bushy tailed. With that young smell. Ready to take on the world.

You refused me in the past, but this time I was going get you.

Me and one of your friends, walked over to you.

He was high of me; he would do anything I told him to.

So he spoke to you. Eye to eye.

He said "It's time for you to try me; you don't know what you're missing."

You hesitated.

"Look, a little won't hurt; you just got to know how it feels. We all do it, even those who don't do it have done it before. Quit being scared! C'mon, take a hit. It won't hurt you."

Your curiosity is eating up your mind…

"Listen, you won't get hooked. Look at me, do I look like a drug addict to you? Only weak minded people get hooked. You're one of the most strong- minded people I know. C'mon, have a little fun; you know you're going places."

Finally, you took a hit of me.

People like you always give in when someone bruises your ego.

And then it begins…..our friendship or maybe better said…our "slaveship".

We meet a few more times at parties, clubs, hanging out at houses and apartments.

I got you giggly. I got you laughing and feeling good.

I got you high, buzzing like a hummingbird.

I am the friend that you love to be around, just like all the others.

You are never alone.

Druggies, usually dope with other druggies; it is just the ritual.

You know how wonderful I am to you.

Then I feel my addiction wearing on you, getting inside you, taking over.

I am your friend called dope.

First, it starts when you don't want to dope in the crowd anymore. You'd rather dope alone.

You cannot understand why you feel so funny when you go two days without me. You hit in the morning. Now it's during the day and you have to do it more than usual.

You wonder, "Am I getting addicted? Nah, can't be!"

The addiction is something that you never felt before. It's like a craving; your body breaks down without it. It's like a never ending marathon; no chance to rest.

When will I rest?

Take a hit of me, that is when you can rest. You need me to make you rest.

Can't sleep it off, walk it off, or shower it off.

You're able to work, household chores, no one can tell, you're paying your bills, you are fine.

I'm cool.

Then one day, a day like no other. You are hungry for me, my dope, my feeling. You don't have the money.

Paid for some of me last time. Took a little out of your bank, but this time you have no money.

What are you going to do?

Well, it's time to do tricks for me, but you needed me.

You had no right thoughts, seemingly no sanity. If you didn't know yourself, you would call yourself….

A FIEND!

O MY GOD!!

AM I A FIEND!!!

I am your friend called dope.

Yeah, we finally got to know each other.

I got you. Took a while, but I got you.

I broke the stallion.

The chemical dependency is like no other. You run to me like a baby.

Your eyes are now blood shot red with a touch of grey. Soon the sores will come, and then your teeth will go bad.

Your appearance will make the brightest light grow faint. You will ruin the prettiest painting, tarnish the beautiful photograph. Learn to live in an image driven world.

You are my slave. All your money comes to me.

I am your landlord. Your insurance policy. I am the most important.

More important than your car, bills, clothes, and family.

That's right.

Lie and steal for me.

When a person is hooked on dope, that person is not the same person as once before.

I came to you as a friend. You know to kick it with, but I came to a lot of people as a friend.

Some got hooked.

Some didn't.

You can never tell who is strong enough. If there really is a such thing.

Some got lucky, or maybe blessed.

We'll never know, but sometimes, even the strong succumbs.

Sex, money, and drugs. The fall of many, men and women. Once you get caught up in them, and you like it, it's hard to let them go.

You'll chase them to them to the ends of the world. It is like a snake eating its own tail. To those who have an addictive personality. These 3 things are highly addictive.

I am your friend called dope.

"I come to you as a friend, but my intention is to make you my slave."

Collapsing

Time seems to go so fast these days.

As if speeding up.

Space shrinking.

Milky Way minimizing.

Cosmos collapsing.

Stars burning out.

Every year the sun seems to sets earlier, faster than what it once did.

And our winters are becoming more non-existent.

And if existence is ending, in short periods.

How much time do we have left?

Can we live? Live not as if in a routine lifestyle?

Wake up, work, sleep, sh_t

But do we have time to do the things that we enjoy

Was life just all work?

Until we grew too old to do it anymore?

Was that called life?

If the walls of time are closing in on us, how will we humans handle this shortened existence?

Maybe the man on the side walk had in right, his sign saying "the end is near".

But mankind still able to squeeze, somehow, a couple of more generations.

Is it mankind's nature to kill ourselves if too many of us populates the earth?

What if there are more people than jobs?

Until something cataclysmic comes along, and wipes a lot of us out?

Are we a mathematical equation? Adding and subtracting?

But yet I remain optimistic.

Special but never forgetting that I can die like the rest.

I am human.

Can you hear my philosophy?

Can you feel my poetry?

Not trying to brainwash you, just want you to vibe on my words for a while.

Such a silly video playing sitcom watching world.

Where are all the smart people at?

They are making deals with AOL, Yahoo, Google, and Microsoft.

Making billions from the silly video game playing sitcom watching world.

I would like to believe in a God that loves me, and this society, and this world, and this universe.

That we have not grown too bored or upsetting

What does it matter to have all the fame, money, and respect in the world?

When the universe wipes its apocalyptic hand over the earth and wipes away everything that once was.

No more fame, money, respect or man's inventions. No history and explorations.

Nothing!

Nothing to give evidence that we were ever here.

Make ground for the new chess pieces to inherit the earth, and everybody will be in judgment.

Every year, more and more historians, intellectuals, and scholars argue the validity of Jesus.

Everybody has their beliefs to believe in, but I remain optimistic as I originally started.

If life is closing in on us, do we make our lives better or do we become more selfish beings?

Well, I think that choice is personal.

It depends on your mind, spirit, and how you are made up.

It is up to you to make your spiritual decision.

The repetitive choices you make, guides you either to or away from God.

Even though the more I age, it seems that selfishness, and hate is somehow part of some people's DNA.

Bad people created to give the good people friction.

If everybody was good, life would be boring and uncompetitive.

Good must have bad to battle, it makes for a good sports event and I guess for the spiritual forces that are watching us.

Wise people know the importance of life, because they knew how to savor.

To the fools, life was fleeting. They never thought that they would grow old

The chess pieces.

I am human

I will take pieces of your beliefs, if I see them fit, add it to mine. Use it to become a better spiritual being.

We are all a part of a bigger puzzle

Some people have the answers, others are totally clueless.

Be careful who you believe, be careful who you listen to.

Prayer will always give you that third eye that sees the truth.

Can you hear my philosophy? Can you feel my poetry?

Not trying to brainwash you, just want you to vibe on my words for a while.

The Coming Of Christ

Jesus came.

He appeared to all of the world.

The Leaders, the policy makers, presidents,
ambassadors, mayors, governors, cabinets, councils,
princes, and parliaments.

There was no more need for authority.

I rejoiced because the Savior has come, and I knew
there was not much time on earth.

The Workers, blue-collar workers, managers, builders,
construction workers, installers, repairmen, carpenters,
fishermen, factory and landscape workers, janitors,
cashiers and low hourly wage workers.

There was no more need for toil and labor.

I rejoiced because the Savior has come, and I knew that
there was not much time on earth.

The Healers, the doctors, nurses, pharmacists,
surgeons, surgical techs, psychologist, psychiatrist,

health officials, and major health pharmaceutical companies.

There was no more need for medications, high blood pressure, cancer, mental illnesses, death, disease, heartache and pain.

I rejoiced because the Savior has come, and I knew that there was not much time on earth.

The law enforcement and judges, the lawyers, paralegals, attorneys, police officers, detectives, prison officials, probation officers, and parole workers, and jailers.

There was no more need for disputes, arguments, crime, or man's law, officials, or judgment.

I rejoiced because the Savior has come, and I knew that there was not much time on earth.

The Military Generals, captains, colonels, privates, corporals, army, navy, air force, marines, fighter pilots, war ships, jets, tanks, missiles, bombs, bullets, grenades, or missiles.

No more covert operations, no CIA or FBI.

There is no more need for killing, battles, destruction or

war.

I rejoiced because the Savior has come, and I knew that there was not much time on earth.

The liars, murderers, rapist, tortures, heathens, conceited, prideful, manipulators, deceivers, those who cause tears, hurt, pain.

Those who did not walk in the ways of the good and righteous spirit.

The evil with thorns, thistles and splinters in their heart. The hateful, the jealous, the envious.

There was no more need for darkness, maliciousness, wrongdoing, and suffering.

I rejoiced because the Savior has come, and I knew there was not much time on earth.

The peacemakers, samaritans, merciful, kindhearted, the patient, the forgiving, the understanding, those who soothe the soul, the joyful, the gentle, the healers, the good.

Those who had love in the core of their hearts.

There was no more need for the light to battle the

darkness, or darkness to battle light.

I rejoiced because the Savior has come, and I knew there was not much time on earth.

The rich, the poor, the intelligent, the wise, the ignorant, the unknown, the famous.

All different types, all different classes.

When they saw Jesus.

In all his glory.

It was so ironic, to some even hypocritical.

Every person wept and fell to their knees, the believers and non-believers.

Those who wanted to go with him to heaven and welcome judgment.

Those who wanted the old ways to remain the same.

Those who chose to be separated from Christ, those who loved and embrace him.

Those who cursed him.

When they saw Jesus in all his glory.

It was so ironic, to some even hypocritical.

Every person wept and fell to their knees. They knew that things would no longer be the same, and the old ways, and the old earth ended.

The preparation for the new ways, and the new earth began.

I rejoiced and celebrated.

I rejoiced because the Savior has come, and I knew there was not much time on earth.

I knew not to hold on to things that were passing, and I knew to hold on to things that were eternal.

The Haters

For every dream that is created in your mind, there is a hater trying to abort it.

Every time you try and shine, there is a hater trying to discourage you and make you quit.

Every city, town, country, and county has haters.

Their purpose is to not make you fly. Show you that you are not a person greater.

Distract your perspective, fill you with lies.

They create mirages; show your faults on a list. Tell you that you are a spotted rock, when you are a glimmering diamond.

An incompetent fool, when in fact you're a brilliant genius. Tell you are unloved, when you have many friends.

Tell you that you are replaceable, when in fact you are priceless.

These are the people of hate, and they will tell you

anything to make you believe you are less than what you are.

If you try and soar, they will bind your wings, and close opportunity's doors.

Take away what you are seeking, extinguish that fire burning in your core.

When you climb, they will try and break the rocks from beneath you.

You have to work twice, three times harder to reach the mountaintop.

Your will must be strong, vision focused, be more that what they view.

They put up signs, barriers, barricades and borders, but never stop.

They, the haters, want to see you lowly. Struggle your whole life, to be the jester to them only.

To always appear weak in their eyes.

If you swim, they will try and sink you. If you try and stride, they will try and trip you.

You must carry on, for your life is a gift given to you.

You must decide, in your lifetime, how far to push, when to stop, when it is done.

Not ruled by some other's haters view, some other hater's rule.

So swim, and stride to your life goals. You only have but one life, and yes, it is a swift one, so cherish it and grow.

Do no spend your time with foolishness and lies.

So the next time you hear words of doubt, keep flying, keep flying.

Hover with the wind beneath your wings, break the haters' binds.

Fly, soar, and glide. Then they will have to look up to you, and no hate will hold you.

A Preacher's Story

Addiction- Persistent compulsive use of a substance known to be harmful.

Addict- to devote or surrender (oneself) to something habitually or obsessively.

Authors Note-Despite the ending of this poem. I believe God can heal all addictions

I was introduced to God at age twelve. Made up my mind to rescue souls from hell.

I found the bible so amazing, found out my new occupation was soul saving.

I found honor in the pulpit, blazed fires in souls that were no longer lit.

I loved God more than anything.

He was my Lord of Lords, my King of Kings.

I felt proud when they called me a preacher. To follow the path of the word they needed a teacher.

All I ever wanted them to know, is how much the

Almighty loved them so.

I was their light in the dark. The silent dog that would not bark.

Their guard from Satan. Show them that Heaven is worth waiting.

I wish I could explain the situation.

It is not worth the explaining, that evil is in the heart of every man.

At the age of 32, I was introduced to methamphetamine.

It crept on me like a snake in the grass. I thought it was a harmless creature that would soon pass.

Then at my least expectation, it bit me, causing a peculiar sensation.

This sensation was different. I could not repent.

It was my God on earth, my pride-full lawyer, my medical doctor, my beautiful nurse.

I knew in my heart it was wrong. Leaving a life that was so far gone.

In my embarrassment I had to be admitted. Labeled in time preacher turned addict. I lost all credibility. My life of liberty.

I told them "my word is my bond" They say cannot be, look at "tracks on your arm."

It is funny how you have to hit rock bottom, to avoid the coffin.

That the only place is up. Find goodness in a soul that is corrupt.

Tell yourself that it is enough. The journey is no longer rough.

I feel somewhat of the man I used to be. The counselor said I was on the road to recovery.

For too long I suffered. They now labeled me "preacher recovered."

Once again, I started the cycle. Reintroducing myself to the bible.

"Sorry I turned my back on you". I felt he already knew.

I did not mean to offend, but somehow I felt already

forgiven.

I read the word every day. Each scripture I faithfully obey.

I am baptized in the Father's love, only sent from the skies above.

Now I am back in the pulpit. In my rightful place I sit.

Rocket launching souls to heaven. Tell sinners where I have been.

That in my trials I am a better man. It was only a test of a spiritual lesson.

In my path of repentance, things grew a bit at chance.

It is funny how life is like a game of chess. The snake caught me at a moment of weakness.

I knew immediately my fate. The viper had me at checkmate.

Even a preacher cannot escape the pressures of life. Feels like a man drowning trying to survive.

I was hoping this day would not come, I was praying. The serpent was behind the brush waiting.

A familiar voice from the past it spoke, like a man at sleep I quickly awoke.

"*Come and seek me I will give you pleasure.*" I quickly kept pace trying to.

The snake spoke, "*Come into my world, my lovely territory.*"

But your desires are only temporary.

"*But do you remember how we used to be bound by blood in holy matrimony.*"

"*Do you remember the sensation along with the pain? As you plunged my needle into your vein.*

Do you remember how you was not the same? How led in ecstasy as you screamed out my name.

Said you would never love again. Your marriage to me has now begun."

I gave my life to God, showed me the right path to trod.

I am no longer your slave, following the path of a knave.

"Go ahead and put it in."

Not sure how the needle got in my hand.

"I am your friend someone who loves you to the end."

God is in me. *"You cannot see God; it is me you see."*

God is here. *"I am nearer."*

God gave my life to live.

"If God is so great then God will forgive. Go ahead for old time sake. Go ahead and admit it. The first time you tried it. You said "that's the shit."

But God…

"He'll understand; he'll give a nod. Just repent after it is done. God seen everything under the sun."

So all I have to do is repent?

The voice grew angry in a vicious tone. I knew from then on I was completely alone.

"Who made you feel good inside. Turn your sorrows to joy when you wanted to cry".

God made the stars, the heavens, and all that is above.

The white snake asks, *"But who do you love?"*

The Lord kept me stable when the world gave me a shove.

"But deep in your heart who do you love?"

The Lord helped me through the pain when I said it was too much.

"But deep in your heart who do you love?"

The Lord is as beautiful as a lovely white dove.

"But deep in your heart who do you love?"

The hand followed by the fingers, the fingers followed by the needle.

Like a flower that lost its pedals. The snake coiled up in my arm. Slithering its way with its wicked charm.

I love God in many and in few, but I cannot be without you.

What If Superman Never Had A Clark Kent?

What if Superman never had a Clark Kent, and there was Superman all the time.

I mean what if Clark Kent never existed? Where would he live, what would be his home?

Lex Luthor and his cronies could easily find out where he lives. Just Google search his street.

How much privacy would he have? How would he get paid?

You think Superman would work for anybody, you think he would have a boss?

How would he shop at the grocery store? Would he pay taxes? Would the IRS bust him for not paying taxes?

I guess Superman would just fly around Metropolis until somebody needed help.

How could he chill at a ball game? If you saw Superman at a bar what would you do?

Hennessy and Coke please…now Supes take it easy you got to fly home.

He probably could not even use the bathroom, imagine that.

How could he have privacy from others?

I'm just saying, as strong as Superman was, he needed a Clark Kent.

The average guy who could be ordinary, have a regular job, live in an ordinary apartment.

He needed time away from being a superhero.

Clark worked the 9 to 5 (these days its 7 to 5 but that's not the point) and had a regular job and lived an ordinary life.

Superman without Clark Kent is like having a job, but having no home to go to.

You would just punch the time clock from work, go to a cot in the back, have a break room, sleep for 8 hours, and punch back in for work the next morning. No time for yourself or your own life.

Everyone needs that freedom of being their own

person, having their own space, the ability to think their own thoughts, and making their own choices.

Everyone needs their time alone.

So if any of you all feel like you're being superhuman, take a moment, and realize that you are just human, with frailties, flaws, like everyone else.

You need time to gather yourself and examine your surroundings. It does not make you weak, it just makes you human.

You cannot be a Superman or Superwoman all the time. Sometime you have to have the simplicity of a Clark Kent, or a Clara Kent, but everybody needs that time to be human.

Don't let life force you to wear a cape and an S on your chest all the time.

Reasons Why I Love My Mother
(Happy Mother's Day).

This poem is dedicated to my mother, Marilyn Simmons.

My face smiles when happy, my face smiles big when you're happy.

T**O**ld me going to church is good, but having a personal relationship with God is better.

To always do your best, and be excellent in all that you do.

When I was in the *h*ospital you stayed with me the whole night.

*E*verlasting, to forever lasting appreciation that I have you as a parent.

When I *r*ipped my jeans you, sewed them back together again.

*S*o many times I messed up, other parents would have given up, but you loved me anyway.

Everyone nee**D**s a good relationship with their mother.

Always tell me you love me before I hang up the phone.

You're aging gracefull**y** and more sophisticated every day.

Do not have a lot of money for Mother's day; all I got was flowers and this poem.

I love you mom,

Happy Mother's Day.

Respect

I never had respect for saving money until I had none.

I never had respect for time until I saw adults grow into old men and women, and saw children become parents with their own babies.

I never had respect for living, until I saw people die, get buried, and within two months, people forgot their name.

I never had respect for prayer until I asked God for help and in time I got an answer.

I never had respect for forgiveness until I made mistakes.

I never had respect for kind people until I was forced to spend a lot a time around rude people.

I never had respect for decency and courtesy until I was surrounded by ignorant fools.

I never valued respect until I saw people being disrespected.

I found that the secret to earning respect is that if you respect yourself, you will gain respect.

The Lord's Discipline

Thorough hunger, I learned the sweetness and blessings of food.

Through poverty, I learned the appreciation of simple abundance.

Through having a home, I was taught patience with people, because I always had somewhere that was mine to go to.

With simple things, I became unstressed which makes the day go longer, and makes you age slower.

From being without, I have learned the greatness of moderation, and that desolate poverty and excessive riches both have their great evil.

I had to experience below to find out that the middle was a truly divine place.

It seems God takes away things so you do not have the urge to chase extravagant things, and become boastful.

These things are done so you can be closer to the Lord, that once you have your riches, or whatever your heart desires you can be grounded.

12 Reasons why people HATE!

1. They usually have an unhappy home, bad relationship with spouse, or children. If hate starts at home, then they hate outside the home.

2. You took your ideas, skills, and talents, used them, and benefited from them. They did nothing with theirs, and are in regret. Ideas and talents die if you do not use them.

3. They have constant negative thoughts to where their every action is a disappointment or a failure. They complain about it instead of fixing it. One bad thought is followed by a slew of others.

4. They do not handle stress well. Stress affects people differently. Some go on a rampage, others pop a cold beer and go to sleep.

5. They don't like it when you're in the spotlight, they feel you are becoming better than them.

6. They want you to be at the same low level as you. When you strive, it constantly reminds them that YOU have a drive and passion that they do not have. It's called envy.

7. It forces them to examine themselves. In a way (non-egotistical tho.. but it's true), when you strive for your dreams and achieve them, you in a sense are better than them. Kills their egos.

8. A funny way of showing that they admire you. They become your biggest fan when you make it through all the storms, and climb those mountains. (I know I said it was funny.)

9. People like picking other people apart to find out what they can say wrong about them, instead of saying what is right about them.

10. They have an illness, injury, or sickness that is forcing them to be unhappy, and not being able to enjoy life.

11. Most people who gossip have no lives of their own that is why they talk about other people. The ones who are being talked about don't have time to deal with it, because they are too busy living and enjoying life. And lastly...

12. It is human nature. There has always been jealous and hateful people. Especially among petty people. It's not going away so deal with it. Keep striving toward your goals.

The Looking Glass

IPods blaring music inside the ear canal.

Vibrating the ear drum back and forth.

Cut off from the surroundings, your own society.

Inside of the world's society, own music of choice.

When will it be? We as a people will become detached
from ourselves?

Detached from society, detached from humanity.

Until we become drunk off of technologies elixir

Drunk off of mobile phones, Xbox's, Nintendo Wii's.

We rather play a video game than spend time with our
spouse.

Social networks are where we visit, rather than talk in
person.

We shop and download online, the computer is our new
retail and grocery store.

Alcoholics of a faster way of doing things, drunk and addicted to technology. The computer being our bartender.

Until nobody talks in person anymore.

An artificial avatar.

Flash animation is our Wal-Mart help line. We order everything through our phones.

They are not even phones; they are mobile computers.

When will it be when we make a choice to replace our talents with the computer?

Until we can make music with the touch of a couple of buttons?

Manipulate our singing voices, where a junior high band can sound platinum?

When will it be when the computer duplicates and replaces our God-given talents?

When will artificial intelligence replace man's intelligence?

The computer is our live entertainment; no real musical

skills are needed.

Until cars can drive themselves, the car is our chauffeur and taxicab driver. Travel in cars that take us anywhere we want to go.

Computers become our best friends. Our psychologists, our number cruncher, our answers to our questions.

I like technology, just like the next person.

But as we look inside the looking glass, what kind of world are we creating?

Are we controlling computers, or are the computers controlling us?

At what point will the question be asked "Is the man running the machine, or is the machine running the man?"

All afternoons spent playing video games

Another time watching reality shows on T.V.

The other time spent watching reality shows on a personal computer.

Watching unpaid movies on our phones at the bus

station.

Downloading and reading free digital unpaid books that the author spent years to write, but not getting paid for his work.

Detached humanity.

We live in a world that we rather spend time with our computer than with our Neighbor.

As we look into the Looking glass what kind of world are we creating?

It is man's geniuses, man's ingenuity.

There is a thin line in a human's mind between master and slave... if not both one in the same.

So obsessed with creating and inventing that our creation becomes the master and we become the slave.

Too humanly ignorant to put a barrier on our machines.

Or maybe to humanly flawed.

In other words, we cannot help it.

To create something greater, accidentally making it

greater than ourselves.

So in love with our machines that we forget it is only a tool.

Slavery was abolished years ago.

As humans, we have a habit of wanting others to do our jobs for us, because we do not want to do the job.

We make computers our slaves, not realizing the more we enslave the machine, the more the machine is enslaving us.

The machine is our Romeo and Juliet wrapped up in circuits, motherboards, glass, and buttons.

We grew too lazy.

The machine became our crutch, our entertainment, our friend that we depend on.

As we look into the Looking Glass what kind of world are we creating?

Are we controlling the invention, or will the invention start controlling us?

Becoming a detached society, detached humanity.

Will the machine be our new books, plays, theatres, and movies?

Nobody talks anymore. Our excuse..."I got a machine just push play...why talk?"

When will the machine be our "Hello's, goodbye, sorry not in yet"

When will they start talking to our children, because we don't talk to our children?

The machine is our babysitter.

The machine is talking to us, it talks to us in the rush of society.

It whispers to us through our downloads, wireless networks, email, broadband, and programs.

Every key punch is a conversation.

Will our Twitter, comments, post, and texting be our new language?

Will that be our new language we learn in grade school?

Everything is fast getting faster, and those who cannot

keep up, suffer, perish, and even die.

The technology machine weeds out those who do not embrace it.

We become mechanical-like as we make more machines.

As we look inside the Looking Glass, what kind of world are we creating?

We must tame the machine like a stallion. We must control the Frankenstein by first making it controllable.

But before you can tame the machine, you must tame the human.

Human lusts, human desires, human greed, and that is more difficult than taming the machine.

When will that time come, when man goes too fast?

Quit thinking. Get tired of studying, learning, regurgitating, and memorizing.

To where we say screw it, just download it into my head.

Meld me to the machine, I have to go to the higher

level.

I don't care about the side effects, No more studying.

I cannot wait, I need the information now. I need the knowledge now. Just download it into my head

Make me one with the machine! I want to be one with the machine!!

When will be machine be a part of our humanity?

When that happens, how much humanity will we have left?

Humanity, "the root word is human".

The human element became too much of a liability.

You have to be human to have humanity.

The more machine, the less the human, and the less the humanity.

How long until that will become a reality?

Detached society, detached humanity.

The Looking Glass.

Forever With You

What is forever?

I am not sure when forever ends, but I know I want to spend forever with you.

Endlessness, infinity, timelessness, eternity, never-ending, always, without end.

How do I describe forever with you?

Is it like seeing the rise and fall of the sun, over and over again, every day shade to black?

Honestly, how long has that been going on?

I want that times 10.

Is it seeing the ocean waves swirl around and around, back and forth?

How long has the oceans been here?

If forever could be measured in oceans and sunsets, that is how long that I want us to be together.

Life is too short to not love.

What little life I have, I want to share it with you. To come home to the same person, to come home to you.

So what is forever?

Is it sunsets while driving on a road?

Is it crashing ocean waves while vacationing on a cruise?

Is it water?

Is it fire?

Maybe just a morning coffee sip.

Sleeping under the covers beside each other at night, and everything in between.

Us and we.

You and me.

Sharing our lives together.

Past, Present, Future

Don't let the past, ruin your present, and the present rule your future.

These three things Past, Present, and Future can be interconnected or totally separated by our thoughts, actions, and choices.

You can let one rule the outcome of the other, or you can let one make the other one better.

All three are largely controlled by your mind, and it is true, that destiny, mostly, is created by us.

10 Reasons Why Women Become Strippers?

Note- These are real dancers (strippers), this is a true story.

It was Tuesday night, 9:15 I was bored, bored to the double "d" bored(d).

I was thinking of something creative to do, so I hopped in the 90 Ford Ranger and started driving around, and I started thinking about Myspace, dag, what can I put on my Myspace?

I turned on Seymour Highway, and Maximus the strip club was down the street, and I was like "Bang!" that's it. I'll do a survey on why women become strippers.

So I went back home got a couple sheets of paper and a pencil, then headed down to Maximus.

I walked in the doors and there were dancers everywhere, I knew a couple of friends who are dancers so I thought hey this would be easy.

I was wondering if any of them were here. I started walking around the club to find my first dancer.

I turned my head and there was Passion, booty *shakin*, entertaining the men.

I saw her last week at Walmart, she was going to some club.

Did not recognize her with her clothes on, fine little ole thing though.

Anyways, she was up on stage doing her thing, I *mozied* up, gave her a dollar and pulled her close.

I told her to come take my survey, she said, "What survey?" I said, "10 Reasons Why Women Become Strippers." She was like, "I'll take it!"

She ended her sessions and came over to me. I asked her to name 10 reasons why women become strippers.

If you cannot give 10 give 5. Also one of the questions was, "What are your thoughts on God?" and "If a man asks for sex, what would you tell him?"

(Let's keep it real) She leaned back and gave me her answers

1. I want to buy a house before I am 25.

2. People "booty shake" in the club for free, why not get

paid for it at the strip club.

3. Fast money, easiest way to make money. I make more in a day than some make in a week.

4. I am confident in my body, if you got it, flaunt it.

5. Pay for school.

Your thoughts on God?

"I believe in God, but I don't go to church. Stripping on Saturday and going to church on Sunday is kind of hypocritical don't you think?"

When a man asks for sex what do you tell him?

"Hell no! Just because I am a stripper does not mean I do not have morals."

Passion answered my questions. I thanked her and she went back to work.

I strolled the club for a while. I bought me a drink of sprite mixed with orange juice and came upon my next dancer.

Her name was Sapphire. She was *chillin* on a bar stool smoking a cigarette. I asked Sapphire if she would take my survey, she said sure.

Give me 10 reasons why women become strippers? Your thoughts on God, and if a man asks for sex what would you tell him?

Here we go, ten reasons.

1. You have a felony, and cannot find a good job.

2. Paying your way through college.

3. They think it is a glamorous life, especially younger girls, but it is such a waste.

4. Girls want men to want them, to desire them.

5. They think the money is good.

6. Grew up in bad families, low self-esteem, and lack of education.

7. Have drug problems.

8. No guidance in their life, no parents around, lack of

support, mother did it before them.

9. Youngness, being young has a lot to do with it, young girls want to be noticed; it is like a dating service to them.

10. Growing up in a poor situation, a lot of girls could not go to college.

Your thoughts on God?

He is what got me through this, without Him I would be on dope or be a prostitute.

He was there when I needed him.

When a man asks for sex what do you tell him?

I am not here to sleep with you or to prostitute you, I am here to entertain you.

Most men who come in here are jerks. They think we are horny freaks or something, but we are not.

I thanked Sapphire for taking the time out to answer

my questions. She was queued to go on stage next and she had to go.

My last dancer was Gage, but I had to wait on her. She had pretty good business, she was entertaining the men, but she promised early on to take my survey.

She finally sat at the bar and I had a chance to catch her. A dude was talking to her. I came up and asked if she was ready, she said yeah.

She told the man she was taking a survey and to come back later, she showed love.

She could have been making money, but she turned her attention to my survey and that was cool.

She downed her drink and started the answers.

10 Reasons why women become strippers?

1. To take care of my daughter.

2. To go to school.

3. Fast money.

4. To get ahead in life.

5. To take care of my sister's family.

6. Make my own work schedule, so I work when I want to, or when needed.

7. Can travel on my job.

8. Get all my bills paid.

9. Get photo shoot opportunities.

10. Meet famous people.

Your thoughts on God?

"I was raised in the church my entire life. I believe you have to have God in your life."

"I feel that you need God to survive."

When a man asks for sex what do you tell him?

"I look at him like he is crazy and ask him what does he mean by that?"

I finished the survey, she gave me a hug, and I headed for the door.

I have to admit that I saw these girls in a different light. Before this, half of me, thought that strippers were women who could not make it on a job.

There were many reasons why they chose to do what they do. I guess that.... ...there was a person behind the dancer.

A soul behind the see-through scantily-clad cloth, leather, bikini strings, and hypnotic sexual music.

They had families to care for, struggles, dreams, like everybody else.

They had no less of a relationship or connection to God than anyone else.

They loved God, and God loved them back.

Above all else they were people. Society treats them less than that, especially men.

They have hearts, and feelings like everyone else.

(End of Survey)

Note

We are so quicker to pass judgment than to send a prayer.

Christians, religious people, and church goers preach so much about how they want to bring people to Christ, but so easily condemn and shun a person who might need Christ the most.

Religious people are usually known to pass judgment.

Who are they, or we, to condemn?

God works on people's hearts that are invisible to you. Only God sees the seen *and* unseen; we do not have that vision. God knows the heart, and hears the personal prayers.

Sometime people got to work things out in their own way and in their own time. Who are we to hold on to our prayers thinking that certain people do not deserve it?

Everyone needs prayer. We have not studied, conversed, worked alongside, or know their history, friends, or families. We have no understanding, or clue, of who this individual really is.

Circumstances sometimes does not tell us the true personality or soul of a person. We have not walked in their shoes or know what is going on in their lives. Yet we judge the person and turn away, instead of praying for them.

Is that ultimately what Christians are supposed to do, to pray for the betterment of someone?

You do not have to be a "holier than thou" Christian, faithful church-goer, or a religious preacher who loves to sermon about hell, fire, and brimstone.

All you have to be is a person who wants someone, and everyone, to rise to their highest spiritual level so they, and all of us, can choose to live a more righteous life.

As They Say...It's All Bullshit

People talk. People have their opinions.

Most opinions are usually wrong or biased, because people rarely research to gain the knowledge to really know what they are talking about.

Some people are just addicted to "Gossip and Drama."

They go on what they think, not how something actually is.

After all…it is just another opinion, like butt holes everyone's got one. This is all you need to know.

Take care of yourself.

Take care of your family.

Keep shelter over your head.

Keep food on the table.

Keep clothes on your back.

Keep your transportation in running condition.

Make your money.

Treat people right. Be a help and not a hindrance to society.

The rest, as they say, is "Bullshit."

It is for talk, tell, show, gossip and drama.

Somebody always got something negative to say no matter how prosperous you are, or how good you are doing in life.

People are going to talk about you whether you are doing good or bad.

So just go ahead and enjoy life the best you can.

No matter how nosy they become.

If you do those 8 things, you owe no one an explanation about how you live your life (Except probably your spouse).

This is just a few tidbits to add.

You may not realize how your kindness affects others,

but I promise no matter how many mean spirited people you encounter, in the long run you will be blessed.

Kindness is often remembered, and doors can be open to you by people that you long forgotten. People may not remember names, but they remember kindness and ugliness.

At the same time don't let people run over you or take advantage of you.

Misery loves company, but misery usually ends up alone.

Try and be a help and not a hindrance to society.

Society can be cruel.

Do not give in to anger. Do not let your anger turn into hate.

Hate turns you into a person full of malice, spite, and jealously.

Vindictiveness and excessive pride, blinds you into thinking that these ways are just and right.

It corrupts the people and things around you.

Ultimately, you accept right to be wrong, and choose wrong over right.

The path of love leads to understanding, it gives wisdom to find happiness in a sinful and complex world.

Find what makes you happy in life, build it abundantly in your heart.

Allow it to carry you through the hard times, because dark times will come and are inevitable.

When people upset you as they eventually will do, you can fall back on those things or people that make you happy.

Finding things and people that make you happy, makes coping in society better.

Negative people think backwards.

They think "That can never happen, that will not happen."

Positive people think forward. They say, "How can it happen? What does it take and how can we make it work?"

Positivity helps make progress easier.

Negative people cause things to stay the same year, after year, after year.

Positive people make it change, to where it is not even the same as it was before.

Negative people have no hope, and kills motivation.

Positive people give hope to others and causes people to get motivated.

Everybody has their opinions, and they are entitled to it.

Usually with opinions you usually have to consider the source.

What is the character and integrity of the person who said it?

So all said and done.

This is all you need to know

Take care of your family.

Keep shelter over your head.

Keep food on the table.

Keep clothes on your back.

Keep your transportation in running condition.

Make your money. Treat people right.

Be a help and not a hindrance to society.

Take care of yourself.

The rest, as they say, is "Bullshit."

It is for talk, tell, show, gossip, and drama.

Somebody always got something negative to say no matter how prosperous you are, or how good you're doing in life.

People are going to talk about you whether you are doing good or bad.

So just go ahead and enjoy life the best you can.

Misery loves company, but misery usually ends up alone no matter how nosy they become.

If you do those 8 things, you owe no one an

explanation about how you live your life (Except probably your spouse).

Fame

Ah fame, the mixture of being noticed in the light of attention, but want to hide in the dark, when everything you do is noticeable, scrutinized, and gossiped about.

When is the famous life personal, when is it private, when does it belong to you, when does it belong to the world, when did you lose choice in the matter?

Would you make that choice again to have fame? Once known you are always known. Fame cannot be so easily thrown off like a robe.

Ah fame, the masquerade, the agony, the ecstasy, the yin and yang, the two sided coin.

Do you really want everyone to know your name?

The favor of being known, the whisper on people's lips, the name at the end of cell phone talks.

People peak when you walk into a room.

The admiration, the adoration, the fawning, the fans, the special gifts, treats, and seats for you.

Ah fame, is anybody truly ready for it.

So quick to have it, but so quick to lose it in certain situations when trying not to be recognized.

Total strangers gazing into the keyhole of your personal life. Giving comments and opinions on someone they never had a conversation with.

Fans, strangers, admirers, onlookers, how they so forget that they know you, but….you don't know them.

You are the magnet attracting everything around you. A device you cannot shut off and on where ever you go.

Ah fame, do you really want everyone to know your name?

Sometimes we miss the blessing, maybe with exception of a few family, friends and associates, of no one knowing your name.

Let's Come Together To Celebrate Juneteenth

Let's put our differences to the side, the bickering
amongst each other.

Let the tensions within subside, let's fellowship with
our sister and brother.

Let's come together to celebrate Juneteenth.

Let not negativity enter the doorway or a jealous bone
enter the building.

Keep the grounds clear of gossip say, let the
atmosphere be free of quarreling.

Let's join, unite, assemble, and come together as one,
for the celebration is but once a year.

Let's have our talent shows, music, bands, dance, food,
and fun. While poetry and gospel singing fills our ears.

Let's come together to celebrate Juneteenth.

Let's hear about our history, from old past to present
day new.

The greatest stories told is our story, of how freedom came to me and you.

Let it be recorded, and witnessed from our ancestors' heavenly eyes, that our people put aside their differences.

Came together with welcoming hugs, encouraging words with arms open wide.

Let's come together to celebrate Juneteeth.

Making Love In The Matrix

You are my serenity.

Quiet oceans, soft sand beaches, and a cool breeze.

My Neo to your Trinity.

Entangled in our own matrix, for our eyes only.

There is no Agent or Morpheus, no plug in the back of our skull to download information.

No special weapons, spaceships, or an oracle talking to us.

All we need is drinking glasses, wine bottle, sheets, and our imagination.

If you can make love to the mind, you make love to the soul, the body, and the sensual.

There is nothing you cannot touch, you cannot find, physical stimulation starts with the mental.

Our Matrix begins, with our imagination.

A radiant fire,

A dark night and salt moon.

We hold hands and hover higher and higher suspended in animation in the middle of the room.

Using our Matrix mind power.

Fast then slow motion ecstasy is the aim.

While making love naked again and again above the flame.

The ceiling opens up and it starts to rain, we never get wet, never putting out the flame.

You are my serenity, making love is only limited by your imagination.

My Neo to your Trinity. Every time we make love, it is a new exploration.

Pinch My Nipples

You are beautiful.

Poetry is in the rhythm of your walk, music in the words that you speak.

European model mixed with the girl next door appearance.

Magical, and amazing.

How could a male and a female create something so lovely?

Surpassing in grace, etiquette, and intelligence.

As if you could never grow old. But even in old age, you would still be exquisite.

Wrinkles and grays place in the right spots.

Showing even more grace, etiquette, and intelligence.

A rich cake made with all the ingredients. With a top and rich middle layer.

I want to be intimate with you, but in my Christian

heart, covered up with lust.

God did not bring me into your life to have sex with you. Make love to you intermingled in fiery passion, passion fire

Maybe to show you how valuable you truly are, or maybe be one of the few men who cares about the balance of your soul, and not the satisfaction of his loins.

Never gossip that I slept with a queen.

Appreciate you, not give into depreciation.

Value you, not devalue you.

You're inside and out a gem with all the right cuts blinding when hit upon with light.

I yearn for you, wanting to personally bathe you with the softest cloth and the perfect honey smelling body wash, massage your feet until you fall asleep.

There are so many things I want to do. It would not be a list, but a book.

I am into you.

I fear my straight forwardness might jeopardize her friendship.

Apprehensive. Another word for afraid.

To make that leap.

Not knowing if you would accept me, or reject me.

So I say nothing, and I ask for one thing and no more.

I was wondering, if you could………...
.... pinch my nipples?

I Go Quietly

I have unlocked the mystery of my question "How do I escape the enslavement of society?"

To not be burdened by an overworked, underpaid, and underappreciated occupation.

I have at last found my niche that was made specifically for me.

Not having to answer to bosses, supervisors, and managers, who hold my hard earned check in the palm of their hand.

To hire and fire whenever and whomever they wish to.

I must perform, entertain, and dance at their every beckon and will.

I am the tiger being cracked by their whips. Their acrobat, trapeze artist, and clown. To loyally follow them, the ringmasters.

The workplace is a circus, to only leave when I am of no longer of any use to them.

They make-up the rules as they go along.

They lie to us telling the rules are for us all, but we are the only ones abiding by them.

We, the workers, run the show. While the ringmasters reap the ticket sales.

Tossed to the side if we miss too many days. Discarded if too many days out sick.

To never speak of the injustice us the workers daily suffer.

Keep tight-lipped and be proud of the meager, barely enough to pay the bills, and better be happy with what you got.

In all this, I have finally found a restful sanctuary.

So with no bow, grand exit, or adieu. I go quietly.

No departure of a roaring fire truck heard blocks away, no snide remarks, no stamp, or tattoo, or imprint of a reminder of me.

No shout out "Remember Me!!"

No handshake, hug, or goodbye.

You will just have to write me off, no longer work here.

How much time will pass before you realize I am gone?

Who knows after a month has passed, who will care?

I am away from here to my new found place.

A new beginning, where I will have no memory of you.

Secretly, I wish and hope you will have no memory of me.

Yes, I Will Love You When You Are No Longer Famous.

(This poem is the response to the poem "Will You Love Me When I Am No Longer Famous")

Baby....

I never cared for the *poppin* bottles, comfortable houses and hardwood floors. Dressed up like high fashion models.

I never cared for the riches, the expensive and the exquisite.

The fine, the lavish, the over the top, the luxury.

The travels, the exotic, the fame, the foreign countries and hotel visits.

What mattered was...

Were you happy with the life we both lived? Were you at ease with the life choices you made?

If something happened and you could not give to a lifestyle that was high paid.

You ask me, "Would you love me if I was no longer famous?"

That you wanted to leave this life behind, somehow be set free.

To again walk amongst the crowd unknown and nameless.

To again be the average, the common, to be loved not for wealth, but simply… for me.

Quiet peace, quiet privacy.

That fame and wealth, trashes, throws, and burns fearlessly.

Again to be left alone to yourself. Without having the phone ring aimlessly,

Ring, Ring, Ring, Ring, Ring.

Baby….

Wherever you go I will follow.

My water is deep, not shallow.

If you want to leave this life, together we'll make the

leap.

We can start tomorrow.

Baby…

We can start anew.

Let the sands of fame wash away with the new.

A new quieter life we can claim.

Just us.

We are family. You and me.

Like peanut butter and jelly.

Baby….

I never cared for the *poppin* bottles, comfortable houses
and hardwood floors.……..…….

Dressed up like high fashion models.

You are at the inner most part of my heart; my core, my
balance, my center.

Fame and vast amounts of money can be let go so

easily as long as we have each other.

To answer your question, Yes, I will love you when you are no longer famous.

When they no longer cheer for you, when they no longer clap for you.

Yes, I will love you when you are no longer famous.

The Crab Syndrome

1. Referring to a community, or a group of people, resembling crabs in a bucket. That when one tries to leave, the other crabs pull them back down.

That if a person tries to excel in life, their community does not help them, and prevents them from excelling or leaving the neighborhood or community.

Describes a way of thinking, best described by the phrase, "If I can't have it neither can you!"

2. An abnormal, dysfunctional, retardation, or disorder in which a community does not help, support, or give assistance to someone of their own community, who is trying to strive. To purposely hinder one's ability to succeed.

Why did you kill that child's dreams?

Laughed when trying to learn, turn your head and walked away when they asked for your help.

Let them fall when you gave no support, then talk

about how much of a failure they are when they fail.

Forbidden to express themselves, words of disappointment rather than words of encouragement.

Why did you kill that child's dreams?

How long will we give into the Crab Syndrome?

Like crabs in a bucket, when one tries to get out, the others pull them down.

How long will we pull ourselves down? How long will we stay in the bucket?

Why did you kill that business owner's dreams?

Never shop at their stores, a store in the community, but not used by the community.

Never buy their products or merchandise. Tell others not to spend their money there, rather close to home.

How can we thrive if we do not support our own businesses, right next door?

How can we flourish if we do not own our own businesses? Go in and steal from our stores.

How can we grow if we take from our businesses?

A wallet full of money, but still take from our stores.

How long will we give into the Crab Syndrome.

Like crabs in a bucket, when one tries to get out, the others pull them down.

How long will we pull ourselves down? How long will we stay in the bucket?

Why did you kill the community's dreams?

Never show up at their meeting, but the first to criticize the meetings.

Gossip amongst each other.

Every event the community tries to have, you find a way to speak negatively about it.

Every fundraiser you say you don't trust them with your money.

If we can't trust each other, who can we trust?

Nothing ventured, nothing gained. No chances, no risk taken, just complaints.

Asked to donate 5 dollars. You reply, "Not getting any of my money."

What's five dollars?

Instead, you go buy a hot dog and soda with it.

What's five dollars? You go by $80 dollar sneakers.

What's five dollars? You go buy and DVD and CD with it.

What's five dollars? You go buy a video game with it. Video games are 5 times the price.

We invest in everything else, but ourselves.

What is 5 dollars for a working community?

Bring up old rumors about people.

Unbury old skeletons, what they used to do years ago. Which has nothing to do with what they are doing now. Which has nothing to do with staying positive

Rather have personal indifferences than communicate.

Want others to carry the burden, while you sit back and watch, then jump on the bandwagon.

Ride upon their coat tails, when they get something started.

Nobody wants to help when you're struggling.

Nobody wants to help build, but everybody wants to help if they see they can make a profit.

You want others to take the lead, who will take the lead?

The sky is the limit.

There are many opportunities. Don't be blinded to think there are none.

If we just stand and watch, we will never get off the ground, but one person cannot pull the load.

It is the people, not the person that makes the difference, but it is that person that can make that first step.

Like crabs in a bucket, when one tries to get out the others pull them down.

How long will they stay in the bucket, how long will we pull ourselves down?

Why did you kill our dreams?

Those who dreamed of becoming a musician, writer, business owner, hair stylist, inventor, chef, computer scientist, politician, entertainer, actor, filmmaker, singer, doctor, architect, banker, entrepreneur, teacher, astronaut, scientist, athlete, congressman/woman, and president.

The sky is the limit.

They are many opportunities, don't be blinded to think they are only one.

You throw a blanket over our neighborhood, and community.

This Crab Syndrome blanket spreads across the community, it makes it to where you cannot see the clouds, bathe in the sun, or reach for the stars.

It is not the people outside the community; it is the next door neighbor.

The person across the street, the people in the house around the corner that is causing it to become dark.

With no light we cannot grow.

We must be the food and light for our community.

Just because you put a blanket over your dreams, does not mean you have the right to cover another's.

How long will we give into the Crab Syndrome?

Like crabs in a bucket, when one tries to get out, the others pull them down.

How long will we stay in the bucket?

How long will we pull ourselves down?

The secret of destroying the Crab Syndrome, is that if we help others get out of the bucket, then eventually, we will all be out of the bucket,

Those who choose to be out the bucket.

We must break the Crab Syndrome mentality.

We must support, encourage and love each other.

We should not discourage the ones who have the potential to become great people, who come from our community.

Thank you for reading my book "The Crab Syndrome."

I am the author of two other books; "The Phoenix's Dying Light" and "The Mustard Seed"

I am the owner of some online websites. My poetry website Southern Poet www.southernpoet.com.

My search engine Wolverine www.wolverinesearchengine.com.

As well as my black history video website Black History Films at www.blackhistoryfilms.com. You are welcomed to check them out.

Antuan Rene' Simmons

Made in United States
Troutdale, OR
05/06/2024

19687729R00086